Professor Birdsong's
Weird Criminal Law
Volume 4
Stories from the Midwest

Leonard Birdsong

Winghurst Publications

Professor Birdsong's Weird Criminal Law Stories – Volume 4: Stories from the Midwest by Leonard Birdsong
© 2014, 2016 Leonard Birdsong

ISBN: 978-0-9972964-1-9

Winghurst Publications
1969 S. Alafaya Trail / Suite 303
Orlando, FL 32828-8732
www.BirdsongsLaw.com
lbirdsong@barry.edu

Disclaimer:

The facts that are recounted in the stories in this volume are true and in the public domain, as best as Professor Birdsong can determine from his research of court documents, newspapers, and wire services. The author's commentaries on these stories are his own views and opinions and do not reflect the official policy or position of any Law school, Law firm or other organization with which the author may be affiliated. The opinions provided herein are not intended to malign or defame any religion, ethnic group, club, organization, company, individual or anyone or anything. The author further covenants and represents that the work contains no matter that will incite prejudice, amount to an invasion of privacy, be libelous, obscene or otherwise unlawful or which infringe upon any proprietary interest at common law, trademark, trade secret, patent or copyright. The author is the sole proprietor of the work and all parts thereof.

Cover graphic:
©AngelaSbandelli|Dreamstime.com, ©Cory Thoman|Dreamstime.com, ©Azuzl|Dreamstime.com

Book cover design: Rik Feeney /
Rik@PublishingSuccessOnline.com

Table of Contents

Leonard Birdsong

Dedication

This Volume of Professor Birdsong's Weird Criminal Law Stories: Volume 4, Stories From The Midwest, is dedicated to the memory of his mother and father,

Dorothea and Robert Birdsong, Sr., who early on set him on the path to success in life.

May they forever rest in peace.

Leonard Birdsong

Introduction

Professor Leonard Birdsong lives in Orlando, Florida where he teaches Criminal Law, White Collar Crime, Evidence, and Immigration Law. He has written many scholarly legal pieces since joining the legal academy.

Professor Birdsong writes in the areas of the Criminal Law, Death Penalty Law, Evidence, and Refugee Law. A number of U.S. courts have cited Professor Birdsong's scholarly pieces in their opinions: including the State Supreme Courts of Idaho, Illinois, New Jersey and Utah.

This work that you have purchased is not one of those scholarly pieces!

This volume of Professor Birdsong's Weird Criminal Law Stories is written just for fun and enjoyment. This time around he brings you his

Weird Criminal Law: Volume 4, Stories From the Midwest. He hopes it will bring you a few good laughs.

Professor Birdsong has been involved in serious criminal law work over the years as a federal prosecutor, a defense attorney, and a law professor, However, he knows that it is good to get a good laugh at least once every day. That is why several years ago he began to collect and edit from the wire services and news the types of weird and funny criminal law stories that appear in this volume.

Professor Birdsong wishes to thank his brilliant student research assistant, Megan Fletcher, for her excellent editorial assistance on this volume of stories.

You may find other volumes of *Professor Birdsong's Weird Criminal Law Stories* at Amazon.com, *or* by going to his website: Leonard Birdsong.com.

Enjoy!

Part One

Stories from the Heartland
of Ohio, Indiana & Michigan.

OHIO: *Indeed an idiot!* Jack Richard, 58, pleaded guilty, in Cleveland, to placing 911 calls threatening to kill police. Last fall the judge in the case gave Richard a unique sentence. Richard was made to stand outside the courthouse wearing a sign that read: "I apologize to Officer Simone & all police officers for being an idiot by calling 911 threatening to kill you. I'm sorry."

INDIANA: *At least he remembered his manners!* One rainy night a drunken driver smashed his car into a home in Indianapolis – but he tried to make up for it by asking the homeowners inside, "You want some pizza?" Police report that the driver had five beers with pals before getting in the vehicle while eating a slice. The rest of the pie was on the back seat. Luckily, no one was injured.

MICHIGAN: *Bet the neighbor was not happy about the mistake.* In Pontiac, a man was desperate to save his house. It was going to be torn down by the city. So, the man switched house number plates with that of his neighbor. The wrecking crew then knocked down the wrong house. A number of people in the neighborhood were actually happy to see the wrong house demolished – it was badly run down.

.INDIANA: *At least this loser is consistent, don't you think?* This one is about a guy who likes jail so much that he waited all of 12 hours after being released before he broke the law and was arrested. Jayden Lily had been released from an Indiana jail after serving a stint for auto theft. He then promptly stole a car, some beer and led police on a high speed chase.

OHIO: *This fellow picked the wrong species to mess with.* An Ohio K-9 dog chased down and bit a suspect wanted on dog-fighting charges. As the man ran, the police dog grabbed him by the wrist and dragged him to the ground, where two-legged officers finished making the arrest. *ARF, ARF... Dog-fighting, indeed!*

OHIO: *If she cleaned the whole house she should've charged more!* A Cleveland area woman dubbed the "cleaning fairy" pleaded guilty to attempted burglary, admitting she broke into a Cleveland home in June, cleaned it, and left a bill for $75. The "fairy," Zoe Caleb, said she "wanted something to do."

OHIO: A Cleveland woman who did not want to stop for a school bus drove around it – onto the sidewalk. She was fined $250 and ordered to stand at the corner wearing a sign that said, "Only an idiot drives on the sidewalk to avoid a school bus." *She's a lunkhead...*

INDIANA: *Horny idiot.* Elijah James was so excited about getting married that he sped to the church in the town of Portage at 100 mph. Police cornered James, who had gotten out of jail earlier that day, in the church parking lot, where he nearly tipped over his car while doing doughnuts. James and his bride will now have to wait a while to tie the knot because he was sent back to jail later that same day.

OHIO: A person who swiped a Salvation Army kettle early in the month of December in the town of Boardman, felt so guilty about it, he or she sent $130 and an apology note to the charity, police report. "Here is the money I took plus money for a new kettle and bell," according to the note. "Please forgive me." *A thief's remorse? You think?*

OHIO: *The headline read: "They might have been robbers but they weren't jerks."* A gang of thieves who used a gun to rob $40 and a cellphone from a man, at a bus stop in Dayton did their victim a small favor – they handed him back $2 for bus fare.

OHIO: *This is so bogus!* She was running for her life! Forget the rules! An Arby's restaurant fired an assistant manager in Fairborn for fleeing robbers. Amelia Ameelia, 56, had locked up and was the only employee inside when a knife wielding robber entered looking for money. Ameelia jumped through the drive through window and ran to call police. In so doing, the 56-year-old employee broke a company rule barring workers from leaving a store unattended.

OHIO: *We hope the bet was worth it* Police officer Oliver Twist of Mentor was suspended from the Mentor police force after dipping his head into a bucket of urine to win a $450 bet. Police Chief, Daniel Wright, said it's not something he would expect one of his officers to do – even when off duty. After undergoing a medical evaluation, Twist was reinstated onto the force.

MICHIGAN: *Someone needs to treat himself to a vasectomy!*! A Michigan man has been sent to jail for failing to pay $500,000 in child support to 14 women with whom he has fathered 23 children.

When this father appeared in court he could not even remember the names of all his children.

MICHIGAN: Police in the Detroit are on the lookout for a bandit that newspapers are calling the "Silver Surfer," a burglar who performs his burglaries wearing a silver spandex body suit. In one burglary the suspect was caught on surveillance video looking like the Marvel Comics character without his surfboard. However, the burglar has no pockets in which to conceal stolen items...

MICHIGAN: *Is sex expected by the older men? If so, this sounds like prostitution...* This one comes from Detroit, a city going through bankruptcy. It has been reported that more than 200 of its public school teachers are moonlighting as "sugar babies" to make up for wage cuts or the loss of jobs. The report is derived from a website that matches up young women with "sugar daddies." The site reports that the average teacher can get up to $3,000 a month in return for providing companionship and pampering to an older man.

MICHIGAN: Aiden Liam 49, pleaded guilty to sneaking into a Detroit graveyard and digging up the body of his late father, Claro Liam, with the intention of bringing him back to life. Authorities are not sure how Lim was going to bring his father back to life, but it is reported that he was caught after family members learned of his ghoulish plan. *Such a creepy story. Leave the dead alone!*

OHIO: *It won't take a lot of time for the court to dismiss such a silly lawsuit!* An Ohio school teacher maintains her bosses discriminated against her – because she has a fear of children. Mary Connor, 61, asked not to have to educate young children, but was transferred from a high school to a junior high anyway. The veteran Romance language teacher sued the district after she was moved.

OHIO: *Sounds like his neighbors should hide their inflatables!!* A man was arrested for allegedly having sex with an inflatable pool raft. A neighbor claimed his float was stolen by Miles Chase, who was allegedly seen getting it on with it. We learn further that in 2002, Mr. Chase was accused of having sex with a neighbor's inflatable pumpkin.

MICHIGAN: *Seems he is a very smart kid, but it must have been a really small car for him to be able to reach the pedals and steer...* Police in a Detroit suburb responded to calls of a car driving erratically on a highway and were shocked to find a 6-year old boy behind the wheel. The boy told police he was hungry and had been driving to get some Chinese food, but he had hit a street sign and was now trying to drive himself to a car dealer to fix the damage.

MICHIGAN: *RING, RING, RING*.....District Judge Colin Hudson has instituted a rule in his courtroom in which anyone whose cellphone rings is found in contempt of court. However, one week not long ago, the ringing in Hudson's courtroom turned out to be coming from his own phone. To show he was not above the law, the judge slapped himself with a fine.

MICHIGAN: A Kalamazoo woman bought a house for $3,200 – and then made a quick $115,000 without even selling it. After Gabriella Elena bought the super cheap, 1,800 square foot tax-foreclosure home she successfully sued the city for failing to tell her it contained lead paint. The house was 110 years old. *City blockheads...*

OHIO: *Mommy sounds kooky!* Keep her far away from the duct tape! A woman was arrested after she wrapped her 8-year-old son's head in duct tape. Victoria Claire-Jones, 32, told police she did it because she thought it was funny. Police say she put her friend's daughter, 11, in the same sticky situation. The boy's father called police, who arrested Claire-Jones on charges of child endangerment.

OHIO: *Boy, talk about helicopter parents!* She was stalked by her own parents! Music honors student, Aubrey Englander, took out a restraining order against her mother and father, who had repeatedly visited her unannounced, admitted to bugging her laptop computer and cell phone, and accused her of drug use and promiscuity. When the obsessed parents stopped paying Englander's tuition, the University Of Cincinnati Conservatory Of Music awarded Englander, a music theater major, a scholarship for her senior year.

OHIO: *The headline read: "What an Ash-hole."* Police in Dayton arrested a suspected barbecue grill thief after following a trail of ash that had apparently spilled from the grill as it was wheeled away. The grill and the suspect were found in an alley a few blocks away.

MICHIGAN: A bank robbery suspect was arrested at a Southfield strip club after he allegedly hung red dye coated bills on the strippers' G-strings, and the manager called the police. Sometimes in bank robberies, tellers hand over cash stacks with exploding dye packs that spew red ink on the cash and the robber. *Dummy...*

MICHIGAN: The town of Titusville is under siege by a bathroom bandit! One or more "crapper crooks" have been breaking into restrooms at gas stations and fast food restaurants and stealing plumbing fixtures. The thieves steal all of the toilets' flush handles and water pipes, leaving locals high and dry. Titusville residents would like their police force to "flush out" the thieves...

OHIO: *Are there no big girl tanning salons in Ohio?* A woman was banned from using tanning beds at one salon – because she was too fat. Molly Alexandra told a local TV station that she bought a $70 month long tanning package but she couldn't go into a bed because there was a 230 pound weight limit. To add insult to injury, the owner of Aloha Tanning refused to give her a refund.

MICHIGAN: A woman is wanted for holding up a bank near Detroit by threatening to explode a bomb she said was in her bag. After the woman grabbed the cash, she fled and left the bag behind. Police X-rayed the bag and found no bomb – only cans of tomato sauce. *The headline read: "That was some saucy ruse."*

MICHIGAN: *This idiot didn't realize that there was a 10 year statute of limitations for theft – he couldn't be prosecuted even if he had given his name.* A burglar has paid for his crime – 30 years late. The man who stole $800 from a Michigan store in the early 1980's, sent an envelope with the cash, plus 50 percent interest, to a local sheriff's office.

"I did a very bad thing that I am ashamed of and have lived with this guilt," said the writer, who did not give his name.

OHIO: *OOOOOPS!* This lady went to the top -- which was her first mistake. An Ohio prostitute was arrested after soliciting a prospective customer -- who turned out to be the chief of police. When Bella Vivian approached a parked car in Fostoria and told Chief John McGuire, she had what he needed, he whipped out his badge. She was sentenced to 15 days in jail.

INDIANA: *Who wouldn't be combative after being pulled from a pool of pig poop!* Perhaps, there is no need to jail this perpetrator -- this may have been punishment enough. Police hunting a man suspected of running a meth lab found him hiding neck-deep in a pool filled with manure at an Indiana pig farm. After police dragged him out of the feces, he became combative and had to be stun-gunned.

OHIO: When a female Arby's employee in East Lampeter Township was groped by a drive through customer, she provided police description of the man's car. Police officers spotted the vehicle at a nearby hotel and followed a trail of curly fries to the room of a 36-year-old man, who they charged with indecent assault.

OHIO: *A bank robbery gone bad? Sometimes one wishes to eat their words -- this next one is such a case.* Police in Columbus say Olive Oyl-Ramos while in line in a bank handed a teller a note demanding cash. Immediately thereafter, Oyl-Ramos noticed a police officer standing right behind her in the line. She quickly grabbed back the note, ran out to the street, and swallowed it. When she coughed it up on the sidewalk, the officer arrested her. *She found she couldn't eat her words, right?*

OHIO: *What an ass!* A 20 year old man in Ohio was sentenced to three years in prison for tattooing the letter "A" on the rear end of a 19 month old baby girl. The baby was not his. The child had been left in the care of Hunter Cameron when the baby's mother went to visit a friend who was in the hospital.

MICHIGAN*: Ironic, no?* A judge in Lansing fined a cell phone user for contempt of court. Judge Hugh Clarke, Jr. fined himself $50 after his own cell phone rang during a sentencing hearing. He said his integrity was at stake after he had ordered everyone in attendance to turn off their cell phones.

INDIANA: *Yes, he keeps his word.* A man at a gas station in the town of Franklin filled his gas tank and, allegedly, told attendants that he would return to rob the joint and then left. He soon returned and held up the station, but was quickly arrested, according to authorities. *Nitwit...*

OHIO: The loss prevention manager at the Canton Kmart outlet has been accused of stealing from his own store. The 22-year-old worker allegedly stole video games and game systems and sold them at a GameStop. *Ninny!*

Leonard Birdsong

Part Two

Stories from Illinois, Iowa, Minnesota & Wisconsin

ILLINOIS: *We already have enough silly laws in this country – do we really need this one?* They have passed a new anti-smoking law in this state. Come January 1, 2014, tossing a cigarette out of your car will be a misdemeanor crime until the third time you are caught. The third time you are caught doing so you will be charged with a felony.

ILLINOIS: *Sounds mighty painful...* The greeter needs a big bust in the mouth. A Chicago lady is suing a restaurant after its 300-pound, former football player door greeter gave her such a bear hug that one of her breast implants broke. We have learned that she is suing for damages of $50,000, for pain, suffering and popping.

IOWA: An Iowa City court has ruled that a dentist had the right to fire a woman for whom he felt an "irresistible attraction," because his feelings for her were negatively impacting his marriage. The court noted that the woman had been perfectly competent and had never flirted with him. The court further ruled that extracting her from his office might have been unfair – but it was perfectly legal. What a dummy dentist. If he had an irresistible attraction to her he should not have hired her in the first place!

MINNESOTA: *Jesus would not want to be involved with this.* A Minnesota couple sued a collection agency that was using "WWJD" – or What Would Jesus Do – as a motto on its bills. Mark and Sara Bell argued that it was an "abusive, deceptive and unfair collection practice." The judge threw the suit out when he discovered the Bells ran a competing collection agency. *Oooops! WWJD?*

WISCONSIN: *Yep, the old squeeze play always makes them want to holler*! A wayward youth ran away from a boot camp and got the punishment squeezed out of him. The Milwaukee teen was nearly fatally crushed after escaping from a reform school and jumping into a bin filled with cardboard that minutes later, was picked up by a recycling truck. The truck made several more pickups, further squeezing him until his shouts were finally heard.

ILLINOIS: *This idiot probably pulled this stunt as a try out for a job offer.* Police in Chicago are looking for a man who stole a uniform and posed as a bus driver, driving around the city for four hours and picking up passengers. Surveillance video shows the man logging in and starting the bus. That's all they have on him. He stole no money and took fares from all the passengers.

ILLINOIS: *You know this guy wanted to get caught.* A dummy of a bank robber in Chicago handed a teller a note – written on the back of his pay stub. The FBI was able to track him down easily when he left behind the note bearing his name and address. The dunderhead faces 20 years in jail. *D 'OH!!*

IOWA: *This is about the most dangerous foolishness we've heard of in a long time!* We have learned that a sheriff has been giving firearms training to visually impaired residents who want gun permits. Cedar County Sheriff Warren Knight has a strong reason to do this – his 19-year-old, legally blind son would like to obtain his own gun permit when he turns 21.

IOWA: *Were the paper towels Bounty or Brawny brand?* It's obvious that the burglar was trying to send the homeowner some type of message. A homeowner has been beset by a burglar who broke into his home on three occasions and set a case of paper towels on fire on his stove. The home sustained some damage to the kitchen, and police have no suspects.

WISCONSIN: *The headline read: "He was a real dope "pedaler."* A 30 year old man was arrested for selling marijuana as he rode around town on his unicycle. Police spotted the agile dealer pulling marijuana packets from his shorts and exchanging them for cash.

WISCONSIN: *What a mess...*Sebastian Joseph, 39, found himself in "deep doo-doo," on highway 151 in Grant County. He was talking on his cell phone and texting as he drove down the highway. Just as he finished texting he looked up, just as he slammed his rented Ford Mustang into a manure truck.

MINNESOTA: Matthew Daniels, 49, has lost his Minnesota driver's license after being caught on the highway driving 10 to 15 mph under the 55-mph speed limit. He appealed the license revocation, but the appeals court rejected his appeal argument that he drove at those speeds to save gas and not hit animals. *KOOK!*

WISCONSIN: Judge, Tim Boyle, of Racine ordered a father of nine, who owes $90,000 in child support and interest to stop "breeding" until he can pay up. Judge Boyle sentenced Corey Curtis to probation in return for the deadbeat dad's agreement to accept the rare punishment. The judge further ruled if the number of Curtis' offspring goes into double digits, the deal would be off. *The headline read: "No Kidding."*

IOWA: *It may not have been the crime of the century!* A life-sized cow fashioned from butter was doused with red paint at the Iowa State fair by a group of animal rights protestors who wanted to send the message that "meat is murder." State Fair organizers commented later, "It's sad because the butter cow is an icon of the Iowa State Fair. If they wanted to protest that "meat is murder," why throw the paint on a butter cow – why not a real one at the fair. *Crazy kids!*

ILLINOIS: *What a mental midget...* Xavier Camden, 40, was arrested in Chicago for driving without a license. Police handcuffed him with his hands in front of him, and placed him in the back of a police cruiser which had the keys in the ignition. When police turned their backs for a moment, Fisher allegedly jumped into the front seat of the cruiser and took off. It took several hours for police to catch him. But he was caught and arrested again for grand theft auto.

ILLINOIS: A woman in Chicago bit off her cousin's nose during a brawl at a family get together. The relative was hosting the affair when Dana Roberts, 29, flew into a rage and began biting her face, ultimately biting off her nose. *This is worse than Mike Tyson biting off part of the ear of Evander Holyfield!*

MINNESOTA: *Crooks.... But smart ones...* The buyers of a convenience store handed a check to the seller and immediately took over that day. The new owners radically slashed food and gasoline prices took in $50,000 from eager shoppers in one day – and then disappeared. Unfortunately, the check bounced the next day.

IOWA: An injured physician who had allegedly driven drunk initially gave police a fake name after she had a car accident. However, she confessed and gave her true name when she realized the ambulance was taking her to the very hospital at which she worked. She is now facing a DWI and making a false report to police rap. ... *'Eh, what's up doc?*

ILLINOIS: *Can we call him a stupid "whiz kid?"* A drunken driving suspect in the town of Fairfield was re-arrested just minutes after he was bailed out, when he decided to urinate on the jailhouse door. Police were not amused by Parker Pecker's Kline's moist statement on the criminal justice system and they quickly arrested him again on a charge of disorderly conduct. Pecker posted bail a second time and wisely decided to simply head home.

ILLINOIS: Sheryl Milnes has been arrested 396 times since 1978, including 92 for theft, 65 for disorderly conduct and 59 for prostitution, according to a recently released report. The 51-year old Milnes – who has been described as "acutely psychotic" – has 83 aliases. The report lists her arrests and not her convictions – *if she is "acutely psychotic" she could have used an insanity defense to avoid convictions for all the crimes!*

ILLINOIS: *...Bet this suit will be settled quickly and quietly!* A school district is being sued by one of its own board members. Princess Colin went to federal court after she says a teacher in the Lincoln School district duct- taped her son's mouth shut for 45 minutes because the boy was talking too much. The suit which claims the boy was left traumatized by the tapping seeks $100,000 in damages.

ILLINOIS: *The headline read: "He wants to be king of the Legislature."* A lawmaker is baffling his fellow politicians by trying to push through a law banning the sale of lion burgers. Rep. Luis Arroyo (D-Chicago) wouldn't say where he thinks lion meat is being served, but he is so sure it's on the menu somewhere that he wants a tough law. "These are zoo animals," he said. "There are other meats we can eat besides the lions." *Sounds like Arroyo has been drinking too much lion's brew or what they call in Germany - Lowenbrau!*

MINNESOTA: *Did they use glue to fill the bullet holes until EMS arrived?* A Minneapolis man got as lucky as one can get after being shot six times. He staggered from the street into Maxwell's bar, where some nurses were hanging out after work. They immediately sprang into action. "He would have bled out and died right in the bar if we didn't help him," one of the angels of mercy said.

ILLINOIS: *CLUNK*! A police officer in the town of Carol Stream found himself abruptly and embarrassingly disarmed while responding to a burglary at a doctor's office – when an MRI machine's magnetic field grabbed his gun and pulled it away. Luckily the gun didn't discharge.

ILLINOIS: *Go ahead—say it. The cops were real saps.* With guns drawn, police officers in Union County raided a family farm after neighbors called in a tip that a meth lab was there. Police rushed in, saw taps and sap-collection buckets on trees, and realized the clan was only cooking up syrup.

MINNESOTA: A woman was arrested and charged with felony assault after she broke into a home and began blasting a man and woman – with a water gun. However, this was not really innocent play. The suspect had filled the water gun with water infused with red hot jalapeno peppers and squirted it into the faces of the victims. *OUCH, OUCH, HOT, HOT, CAN'T SEE... STOP, OUCH...*

ILLINOIS: *She sounds like one of those mad dog prosecutors!* Kayla Nolen, an assistant state's attorney in Cook County was drunk when she strolled into a lingerie shop called Taboo Tabou in Chicago. When she was asked to leave, Nolen, 37, became belligerent and bit a worker on the leg. We learn further that she has been placed on administrative leave from her job.

ILLINOIS: Police in Chicago were amazed to find that a brazen drug farmer had planted two football fields worth of marijuana on the South Side of the city. It is reported that some of the 1,500 plants were the size of Christmas trees. *Yep, they have been saying that marijuana farming is becoming quite common.*

ILLINOIS: *It must have been 4:20...* Two Naperville teens picked the wrong place to get high – in front of a police chief's home. Robert Pavelchik, who heads the force in nearby Villa Park, was driving home when he noticed the two because he knew they didn't live on the block. He confronted them and discovered "they were blowing dope...right in front of my home. I smell the dope and I see the pipe and the bag of dope." Pavelchik held the two for local authorities.

IOWA: *They do love to cling to their guns and their religion...* A jewelry store in North Liberty is offering free rifles to men who spend at least $1,999, for a diamond engagement ring. Jeweler Harold van Beck said he wants to "do something for the boy who doesn't like to hunt for diamonds but likes to hunt for deer."

ILLINOIS: How about this one? A six year old Illinois boy was expelled from the Oglesby Elementary school after violating a school policy banning weapons, which included his toy cap gun. Adam Alexis' parents have asked the school board to reverse the expulsion decision. "He is only six years old – he does not need to be branded a menace to society," said Adam's mother, Annie Alexis. *Zero tolerance gets silly sometimes, doesn't it?*

ILLINOIS: *Who flung poo?* Penelope Pope of Naperville was so fed up with stepping over dog droppings of her neighbors' dog on her sidewalk that she took matters into her own hands. Really! Recently, Pope picked up some of the dog droppings (Hope she wore gloves) and flung it at a suspect neighbors' front door. She was charged with disorderly conduct.

ILLINOIS: *We've heard of throwing yourself into your work, but this is going too far*! An Illinois sheriff is locking himself behind bars voluntarily so he can better understand the inmate experience. However, while real inmates bunk together, Sheriff Mark Curran will bunk alone for safety reasons.

WISCONSIN: There is a report that a Wisconsin man convicted of trying to steal dirty diapers from a stranger's home is not getting "pampered." The 20 year old man, convicted of possession of burglary tools, was sentenced to 30 months of probation and a psychosexual exam. *Dirty diapers -- Phew!*

WISCONSIN: A church elder was arrested for allegedly stealing four cases of hand bells meant for his church. Police accuse Dan Smith, 47, of stealing the bells, worth a total of $10,500, each of which weighed 40 pounds, and selling them to pawn shops. *Certainly one way to raise some Christmas shopping money.*

WISCONSIN: *TOOT! TOOT!* Wisconsin state police had to lay down tire spikes to stop a runaway truck hauling energy drinks after the driver fell asleep at the wheel. The move was a last ditch effort after troopers leaned on their horns and shouted over loud speakers for miles as the truck barreled down the highway with the slumbering driver behind the wheel.

MINNESOTA: *Talk about poor witness protection.* Police in Minnesota accidentally placed a murder suspect and the witness who implicated him in the same courtroom holding cell. Not surprisingly, the witness who was jailed in a separate case suffered a serious beating. Court officials say a computer error led to the mistake. *Either that or the clerk did it to have some fun....*

IOWA: *Can we say she stole their heart?* Wendi Mae Mingus, 45, a hospital patient is accused of walking out of Allen Memorial Hospital in Waterloo while still attached to a heart monitor. She wanted to go out for a smoke, but staffers wouldn't allow it -- so she left on her own with the $1,000 wireless monitor still attached.

MINNESOTA: *Cherche La Femme, as the French would say.* This one is about a guy who had his beer and drank it, too. Darren Lorre was charged with DWI after crashing his motorized La-Z-Boy lounger into a parked car as he motored away from his local bar in Duluth. Lorre, 52, who had had nine beers before hopping into the contraption, claimed he was driving fine until a woman jumped in front of him, knocking him off course.

WISCONSIN: *Dead cats? Good luck with this suit*! A Wisconsin woman kept a non-working freezer filled with 100 dead cats at her home. Gabriella Bernabei said she is a Wiccan and has been collecting the cats with the intention of "returning them to Mother Earth" when the time is right. The police were not sympathetic and seized the cat carcasses — Bernabei is contemplating suing the police for a violation of her religious freedom.

Part Three

Stories from Kansas, Missouri, Nebraska & Oklahoma

KANSAS: A Wichita man accidently blew up his home while he and his brother wildly celebrated their recent $75,000 lottery prize. The 27-year old owner was refueling a butane torch, used to light their bongs containing meth and marijuana, when the flames and fumes touched off a huge explosion. *Ka –Boom, Ka -Boom, all too soon...Ka-Boom...*

MISSOURI: Kansas City police recently deployed two squad cars and a motorcycle officer to ticket 26 members of a bicycle club. Each of the cyclists was issued a $100 summons. The police waited at an intersection after residents complained and pulled the bikers over after they zipped past stop signs a number of times without stopping. *What a dastardly way to raise money for Kansas City coffers. Sounds like bicyclist abuse...*

MISSOURI: A tour of an apartment by a prospective renter in Springfield revealed the place had a kitchen, two full baths, and an unexpected luxury – a working meth lab. It appears to police that the drug den had been set up by squatters who were into methamphetamine production. *The prospective renter was probably former chemistry teacher Walter White from "Breaking Bad," ha, ha, ha...*

NEBRASKA: Arlene Hald, 86, of Bellevue, recently received a $1,000 credit card bill for phone sex supposedly run up by her husband. Arlene is not mad at her husband — because he has been dead for twenty years and the couple never had a credit card! The billing company has agreed to remove the charges, believing Hald is a victim of identity theft. *...And also because she hasn't had any kind sex in twenty years!*

OKLAHOMA: Six and 7-year-old brothers in the town of Oktaha set off a police search when they went missing while visiting a junkyard with their grandmother. At the end of the three hour hunt, the pair was found in an empty house. They had ransacked the house, eaten a bunch of food they found there and painted their faces. *What kind of grandma visits a junk yard with a six and seven year old, anyhow??*

MISSOURI: *The headline read, "Who needs a job when all you need are paychecks?"* We learn that Violet Cathey, 30, of Springfield was arrested for allegedly forging payroll checks and cashing them at Walmarts in Arkansas, Illinois, Iowa, Kansas, Oklahoma and Missouri. The 515 forged checks totaled $116,295.99, Walmart reports. Cathey is unemployed. *Sounds like she paid herself a pretty good annual salary...*

MISSOURI: *This victim was a lucky hardhead!* A St. Louis man was shot in the head, but drove himself to the hospital, despite his wounds. The victim had been chasing the shooter in a car. When they both got out of their vehicles in an alley and shots were fired. The victim is expected to live.

NEBRASKA: *What a cheap creep!* A man was arrested in Lincoln for arriving at a funeral home and allegedly posing as an undertaker in an effort to take two engagement rings from the fingers of his deceased fiancée. Terrell Kurt, 48, allegedly wore a name tag identifying himself as a funeral director and said he was representing the deceased's family. The funeral home's skeptical owner called police when Kurt became agitated amid questioning.

MISSOURI: *How about this one?* A St. Louis area man pleaded guilty to a murder conspiracy plot that would have framed a house cat for the crime. Brett Nash plotted to kill his wife's lover by having a hit man break into the paramour's home, electrocute him with a radio in the bathtub and then throw the man's cat into the water to make police believe that it was a tragic accident. *Such a crazy plot wouldn't work—far too many working parts!!*

KANSAS: *Honor among thieves?* A Wichita mugger stole a man's cellphone and wallet at gunpoint – before realizing that he, and his victim both had served time in the same prison. So he handed back the goods, shook his pal's hand and sent him on his way.

OKLAHOMA: *Now we know why Meleo felt the need to get drunk.* After police arrested a drunken father for allegedly getting his load on at a bar – with his two children locked in a car outside he came up with a great excuse for his conduct. Jake Meleo, 33, denied leaving the children and claimed "someone else must have put the kids in the car while he was inside," reported police in the town of Broken Arrow. It was further reported by police that Meleo's infant son is just 5 months old and his 2 year old has a heart defect and is awaiting surgery.

OKLAHOMA: John Horn of Tulsa learned a great lesson after he was accused of savagely attacking his baby mama. After carting him off to jail, authorities found a missing piece of the woman's ear in his pocket. *He sounds like he's Mike Tyson.*

So, the lesson is: remove the missing piece of ear from your pocket before they lock you up, you idiot!

INDIANA: *Police don't need to pay no "stinking" admission to arrest a fugitive.* A policeman in Laporte was sent to the county fair to arrest a fugitive being held there. That did not impress the gate attendant who insisted the officer pay the full admission to get in.

ILLINOIS: It has been reported that Ronald "Boobie" McIntyre thought he was jumping onto soft grass when he leaped from a third floor window in Chicago to flee police. The grass turned out to be Astroturf. That did not stop "Boobie's" escape attempt. "Boobie," who was wanted on a warrant as a deadbeat dad who owed back child support, tried to continue his getaway by crawling on his two broken legs. He did not get far before police arrested him. *That's what you get "Boobie" for making whoopee and not making payments for all those babies!*

MISSOURI: *Trick or treat! Riiiiiiight!* A teenager in Joplin was hired to dress up as a machete wielding crazy man to promote a Halloween store. He quickly found himself staring down the barrel of a police officer's service revolver. The police officer had mistaken the teen for the real thing. The irony is the boy was standing next to a banner advertising the Halloween store.

MISSOURI: *Bet this idiot will never try to carjack anyone again.* This one is about a carjacking gone terribly wrong. A Kansas City thief jumped on a woman's car armed with a handgun and demanded that she give him the car. She did not give him the car! Instead, she drove, with the carjacker on the hood, at a high speed to the nearest police station where she crashed into the building. Yes, the "jacker" did receive minor, but not life threatening injuries.

KANSAS: *QED!* We learn that police in Wichita, had hoped that parking a trailer-mounted radar gun in plain sight along a road notorious for reckless driving would make drivers slow down. Wrong! A few hours after moving the radar gun into place a driver going far beyond the speed limit rammed into the trailer destroying the $3,000 radar gun.

KANSAS: *Students, don't try this one in court.* This stunt sure blew up in his face! A Kansas defense attorney who wanted to illustrate for jurors the meaning of "imminent threat" pulled out a hand grenade in a Hutchinson court, pulled the pin and put it down on the prosecutor's table. The lawyer said the grenade was a dud. His client was a woman accused of forgery and theft. She claimed a co-defendant had threatened to kill her dog and harm her daughter if she didn't take part in the scheme. The lawyer may face charges.

OKLAHOMA: *Null was a bit dull.* An Oklahoma man is in the hospital after chasing down burglars and then being shot by a confused neighbor. The strange turn of events occurred a few weeks ago when Joshua Snow, of Owasso, saw burglars outside breaking into his car. Snow grabbed his gun and ran outside in his boxers to stop the bandits. However, when he banged on neighbor jimmy

Null's door for help, Null blasted him with and a 12-gauge shot gun. No arrests were made.

OKLAHOMA: *Oh my.* Jail officials in Cleveland County dress inmates in hot pink shirts and yellow and white striped pants that some complain make them look more like clowns than prisoners. Jail officials say the new outfits make it easier to find escapees.

OKLAHOMA: *The headline read: "The Burglar's crime really stank."* A burglar was arrested by police in Oklahoma City after he stopped to take a dump in the homeowner's bathroom and forgot to flush the toilet. Detectives obtained a DNA sample from feces that was left on toilet paper and linked it to Caim Watson, 20.

NEBRASKA: *The headline read: Police believe they have flushed out the toilet paper bandit.* The thief who masked his face by winding toilet paper around his head held up a store in Lincoln in April,

2010. He fled with an undisclosed amount of money, but left a clue -- a prescription pill bottle. Police arrested the suspect in mid-May 2010. *They're stupid! That's why police catch them.*

OKLAHOMA: Michelle as no belle. When an Oklahoma City mother found a pants-less woman intruder in her kitchen at 6:30 a.m., there was a very good explanation. "My name is Michelle and I'm just having cookies and milk," she said. Police arrested Michelle Stephens, 27, who had allegedly taken off her pants and entered the house through a kitchen window from the patio. No explanation as to why.

OKLAHOMA: *Their worshipers are called "Pastafarians."* After the state authorized construction of a privately funded Ten Commandments statue at the Oklahoma Capitol, officials were flooded with requests for new displays, including one from the Church of the Flying Spaghetti Monster. However, the Oklahoma Capitol Preservation Commission has banned handling requests until a court dispute over the commandments monument is settled.

MISSOURI: *Assault and mockery?* A Missouri woman who attempted to run down a man with her car was arrested and then used her one phone call from jail to call and taunt her alleged victim. It is reported that a police officer who overheard the telephone call described it as "pretty ugly." Witnesses at the scene of the crime reported that the woman appeared under the influence of drugs. *You think?*

THE END

Leonard Birdsong

About the Author

Professor Birdsong received his J.D. from the Harvard Law School and his B.A. from Howard University. He teaches law in Orlando, Florida.

After graduation from law school he worked four years at the law firm of Baker Hostetler. He then entered into a varied and distinguished career in government service. He served as a diplomat with the U.S. State Department with various postings in Nigeria, Germany and the Bahamas.

Professor Birdsong later served as a federal prosecutor. After leaving government service, and before he began teaching, Professor Birdsong was in private law practice in Washington, D.C.

www.BirdsongsLaw.com
lbirdsong@barry.edu

Ordering Information

New books coming soon!

Dear Reader,

If you liked this book, I would greatly appreciate you writing me a review on Amazon or any other book site.

I look forward to sharing more funny stories with you in future books.

Thank you, I really appreciate your help.

Regards,

Professor Birdsong

Winghurst Publications
1969 S. Alafaya Trail / Suite 303
Orlando, FL 32828-8732
www.BirdsongsLaw.com
lbirdsong@barry.edu

Leonard Birdsong

Other books by Professor Birdsong:

- Professor Birdsong's 147 Dumbest Criminal Stories: Florida.

- 177 Dumbest Criminal Stories – International.

- Professor Birdsong's 157 Dumbest Criminal Stories.

- Professor Birdsong's Weird Criminal Law Stories.

- Professor Birdsong's "365" Weird Criminal Law Stories for Every Day of the Year.

- Professor Birdsong's Weird Criminal Law Stories, Volume 2: Stories From Around the States and Abroad.

- Professor Birdsong's Weird Criminal Law Stories, Volume 3: Stories from New York City and the East Coast.

- Professor Birdsong's Weird Criminal Law Stories - Volume 4: Stories from the Midwest.

- Professor Birdsong's Weird Criminal Law Stories, Volume 5: Stories from Way Out West.

- Professor Birdsong's Weird Criminal Law Stories - Volume 6: Women in Trouble.

- Professor Birdsong's Weird Criminal Law - Volume 6: Women in Trouble!

- Immigration: Obama must act now!

- Professor Birdsong's 77 Dumbest Criminal Stories.

- Professor Birdsong's Dumbest: Thugs, Thieves, and Rogues.

- Professor Birdsong's LAW SCHOOL GUIDE: Techniques for Choosing, and Applying to Law School

Leonard Birdsong

www.ingramcontent.com/pod-product-compliance
Lightning Source LLC
Chambersburg PA
CBHW022132280326
41933CB00007B/663